CAMBRIDGE LIBRARY COLLECTION

Books of enduring scholarly value

Travel and Exploration

The history of travel writing dates back to the Bible, Caesar, the Vikings and the Crusaders, and its many themes include war, trade, science and recreation. Explorers from Columbus to Cook charted lands not previously visited by Western travellers, and were followed by merchants, missionaries, and colonists, who wrote accounts of their experiences. The development of steam power in the nineteenth century provided opportunities for increasing numbers of 'ordinary' people to travel further, more economically, and more safely, and resulted in great enthusiasm for travel writing among the reading public. Works included in this series range from first-hand descriptions of previously unrecorded places, to literary accounts of the strange habits of foreigners, to examples of the burgeoning numbers of guidebooks produced to satisfy the needs of a new kind of traveller - the tourist.

Narrative of a Recent Imprisonment in China after the Wreck of the Kite

Narrative of a Recent Imprisonment in China after the Wreck of the Kite (1841) is an autobiographical account, written by the merchant sailor John Lee Scott, of his 'shipwreck and subsequent imprisonment in the Celestial Empire' in 1840, during the First Anglo-Chinese or so-called 'Opium' War. In eight chapters, Scott describes leaving South Shields in the *Kite*, 'a beautiful brig of 281 tons' for Singapore in order to 'carry stores to the British fleet destined for China'. Scott recounts how the *Kite* was capsized on its way to deliver supplies to the British fleet based around Chusan, and how he and other crew members, after being washed up on the island of Ningpo, were captured by the Chinese and held prisoner for five months. Scott's *Narrative* provides an interesting insight into British perceptions of the Chinese during the Anglo-Chinese conflicts of the nineteenth century.

T0382152

Cambridge University Press has long been a pioneer in the reissuing of out-of-print titles from its own backlist, producing digital reprints of books that are still sought after by scholars and students but could not be reprinted economically using traditional technology. The Cambridge Library Collection extends this activity to a wider range of books which are still of importance to researchers and professionals, either for the source material they contain, or as landmarks in the history of their academic discipline.

Drawing from the world-renowned collections in the Cambridge University Library, and guided by the advice of experts in each subject area, Cambridge University Press is using state-of-the-art scanning machines in its own Printing House to capture the content of each book selected for inclusion. The files are processed to give a consistently clear, crisp image, and the books finished to the high quality standard for which the Press is recognised around the world. The latest print-on-demand technology ensures that the books will remain available indefinitely, and that orders for single or multiple copies can quickly be supplied.

The Cambridge Library Collection will bring back to life books of enduring scholarly value (including out-of-copyright works originally issued by other publishers) across a wide range of disciplines in the humanities and social sciences and in science and technology.

Narrative of a Recent Imprisonment in China after the Wreck of the Kite

JOHN LEE SCOTT

CAMBRIDGE UNIVERSITY PRESS

Cambridge, New York, Melbourne, Madrid, Cape Town, Singapore,
São Paolo, Delhi, Dubai, Tokyo

Published in the United States of America by Cambridge University Press, New York

www.cambridge.org
Information on this title: www.cambridge.org/9781108013802

© in this compilation Cambridge University Press 2010

This edition first published 1841
This digitally printed version 2010

ISBN 978-1-108-01380-2 Paperback

This book reproduces the text of the original edition. The content and language reflect
the beliefs, practices and terminology of their time, and have not been updated.

Cambridge University Press wishes to make clear that the book, unless originally published
by Cambridge, is not being republished by, in association or collaboration with, or
with the endorsement or approval of, the original publisher or its successors in title.

NARRATIVE, &c.

Drawn by W.J.Huggins.

Engraved by W. Lee.

NARRATIVE

OF A RECENT

IMPRISONMENT IN CHINA

AFTER THE

WRECK OF THE KITE.

BY JOHN LEE SCOTT.

LONDON:
W. H. DALTON, COCKSPUR STREET.
1841.

LONDON :
PRINTED BY G. J. PALMER, SAVOY STREET, STRAND.

TO THE

RIGHT HONOURABLE JOHN PIRIE,

LORD MAYOR OF LONDON,

THIS NARRATIVE

IS,

WITH HIS LORDSHIP'S PERMISSION,

RESPECTFULLY DEDICATED

BY

HIS OBEDIENT HUMBLE SERVANT,

JOHN LEE SCOTT.

PREFACE.

My only apology for launching this unvarnished narrative upon the world is, that, after my return to England, I wrote for the amusement, and at the request of my friends, a short account of my shipwreck and subsequent imprisonment in the Celestial Empire; and considering that my sufferings and adventures would at this time create an interest with the public at large, they have strongly urged me to publish this narrative. This I have ventured to do, hoping that the faults may be overlooked, and all indulgence shown to a young merchant sailor.

London, Nov. 16, 1841.

CONTENTS.

CHAPTER I.

CHAPTER II.

CHAPTER III.

CHAPTER IV.

CHAPTER V.

CHAPTER VI.

CHAPTER VII.

CHAPTER VIII.

NARRATIVE,

&c.

On Monday the 8th July, 1839, I left
Shields for Bordeaux in the Kite, a beautiful
brig of 281 tons, commanded by Mr. John
Noble ; built by, and belonging to, Messrs.
T. and W. Smith of Newcastle. We arrived
at Bordeaux after a three weeks passage, and
lay there for two months. Sailed from
thence on the 16th October for the Mauritius, with a cargo of wines, and arrived there
after a passage of ninety-three days. Here
we remained a month, and having landed
the wines, sailed from thence to Madras

B

in ballast ; where the vessel was taken up by government, to carry stores to the British fleet destined for China : we then sailed for Trincomalee, at which place we took in some more stores, and then sailed for Singapore ; where, on our arrival, we found the fleet had sailed several days before for Macao.

Whilst we lay at Singapore, the Melville 72, Blonde 42, and Pylades 18, arrived, and we received orders to sail for Macao immediately, at which place we arrived after a short passage, but were still behind the fleet, it having sailed some days before for Chusan. We received orders to follow it to Buffalo Island, where there was to be a man of war cruising to give us farther directions; but when we arrived at this island we found no vessel of any kind ; and as we had had a very quick passage, Mr. Noble was afraid to proceed any further, as perhaps we might have passed the fleet, and arrived before it. We therefore brought the ship to an anchor, and lay there till the next afternoon, when the Melville and a transport arrived, upon which we got under weigh, and followed the Melville up to Chusan, where we arrived the day following, and anchored in the outer roads. We found the town in the possession of our own troops, who had taken it the day previous to our arrival: so that if we had not stopped at Buffalo Island, we should have been present at the attack; we heard the firing, and saw the blaze of the burning town whilst on our passage up.

The men-of-war junks which had fired on the Wellesley presented a most wretched appearance, being deserted — some sunk, and others with their masts shot away; and where a shot had struck the hull, it had not only passed completely through the vessel, but also through one or two houses ashore. There were not many Chinese to be seen, and the few that were still in the town, appeared of the very lowest grade. The town and harbour presented, nevertheless, rather a lively spectacle, as boats were constantly passing between the ships and the shore, disembarking troops of varied dress and nations. Two camps were very soon formed, one overlooking the town, and the other on a hill commanding the entrance into the harbour. Sickness soon began to make its appearance amongst the troops, particularly the Company's native regiments, brought on, I think, by inactivity, and by the dreadful smells of the town, as well as the effluvia arising from the imperfectly buried dead of the Chinese; whilst those who were on board ship, constantly at work, and yet drinking the same bad water, were not affected in nearly so serious a manner.

We lay at Chusan for about a month; during which time Admiral Elliott and Commodore Bremer were several times on board of the Kite; and approving of her, all the stores were taken out, and four 32 pounders were put in the hold, as many Chinese guns as we could obtain, seven two-tun tanks, and between 30 and 40 water casks, all for ballast. After this we received six 12 pound carronades, seven marines, five first-class boys, from the Melville ; and Lieut. Douglas R. N. came and took the command. Our crew at this time consisted of the master, Mr. Noble ; the mate, Mr. Witt ; and us four apprentices viz.—Henry Twizell (acting as second mate), Pellew Webb, Wm. Wombwell, and myself ; one Englishman ; an Italian ; and a Manilla man; ten Lascars; and our cook, who was a native of Calcutta, but not a Lascar ; Lieut. Douglas, with the seven marines, and five boys, from the Melville, making in all thirty-three. Mrs. Noble and her child, a boy of about five months old, were also on board.

A short time after Lieut. Douglas hoisted his pennant, we sailed with despatches for the Conway 28, which with the Algerine 10 gun brig, and a small schooner called the Hebe, was surveying the Yeang-tze-keang river, and the adjacent sea. In sailing up this river, we found the charts very incorrect, and at last got on a bank, where we

remained for several days until the Conway
and the other vessels arrived. We had
passed these vessels whilst they were lying
at anchor, in one of the numerous creeks at
the entrance of the river. The schooner
drawing the least water came and assisted
us off; and as the Kite drew ten feet water,
she was of little use in surveying; we
were therefore sent back on Saturday, the
12th of September, 1840, with despatches
for Chusan. One marine and a boy
died of dysentery whilst we were on the
bank.

We brought up that night, and got under
weigh next afternoon; anchored again at
dusk, and very unfortunately, just before day-
break, our jolly-boat broke adrift, and was
carried away by the tide. The gig was
manned, and sent after her, and we followed
in the vessel, as soon as we could get our
anchor: we picked up both boats, but not
without a great deal of trouble; the gig we
hoisted up on the starboard quarter, and the
jolly-boat was towed astern. We anchored

again at night, and next morning started
with a fine fair wind, expecting to be at
Chusan in a day or two. At this time all
the marines but one, two of the first-class
boys, and Webb and Wombwell, were ill of
the dysentery, leaving very few hands to
work the ship.

At nine o'clock on Tuesday morning, the
15th of September, I was relieved from the
wheel, and went below to look after Webb
and Wombwell, and to get my breakfast.
About half past eleven, whilst attending
on the sick, I heard the master order the
anchor to be let go. I immediately jumped
on deck, ran forward, and let go the stop-
per; the vessel was now striking heavily
aft, all the chain on deck (about sixty
fathoms) ran out with so much velocity that
the windlass caught fire. The vessel being
by the stern, and catching the ground
there, the anchor holding her forward, she
could not get end on to the tide, and was
consequently broadside on, and as it was
running like a sluice, she was capsized in a

moment. When the anchor was let go, Twizell and I ran aft, let go the main top-gallant and top-sail haulyards, and were clewing the yards down with the larboard clewlines, when I felt the ship going over. I directly seized hold of the main topmast backstay, and swung myself on to her side, as she was falling : Twizell caught hold of one of the shrouds of the main rigging, and did the same. At this moment I suppose Mr. Noble to have been thrown over-board—I heard him call out to his wife, " Hold on, Anne," but did not see him, and the tide must have carried him away, and of course he was drowned.*

My first thought now was for the sick people down below, who I feared must all be drowned, as the vessel was completely on her side, and her tops resting on the sand. On looking aft, I saw a person strug-gling in the water, and apparently en-tangled amongst the sails and rigging; I got the bight of the mainbrace and threw to him, and with some difficulty hauled

* Note 1.

him on board; but he was only saved then to die a lingering death at a later period at Ningpo. On looking round, I was re_joiced to see the sick people (who I had concluded were all drowned) crawling up the fore and main-hatchways, and immediately assisted them to get on the vessel's side; the greater part were nearly naked, having been lying in their hammocks at the moment she capsized, and out of which some were thrown. I now saw Lieutenant Douglas and the mate dragging Mrs. Noble into the jolly-boat, which had dropped alongside; the two Lascar cabin-boys,* who were in the boat, were casting her adrift; she was full of water, and likely to capsize every moment. I threw my knife to them to cut the towlines, and they, having ef-

---

* These two boys told me, when in prison at Ningpo, that when the brig upset, everything in the cabin fell to the starboard side, where the child was sleeping; that they could not get out at the door, but got out at the skylight, leaving the poor baby to its fate, and got into the boat, which was then on the starboard quarter.

fected this, were swept away, Lieut. Douglas calling to us to cut away the long-boat, which was still on deck. The time between the first going over of the ship, and the drifting away of the jolly-boat, was only three or four minutes, though by this account it may seem to have been much longer.

The gig, being hoisted up on the starboard quarter, was lost to us when the ship fell over, and we could not cut away the long-boat from the manner in which the guns were hanging : we, however, contrived to cut the foremost lashing, and made her painter fast to the main rigging, hoping she would fall off, and that it would hold her. The tide was now rushing down the hatchways : in a short time the boat fell out of the chocks, but the strength of the tide was so great that the line, or painter, snapped, and she was carried away. The weight of water in the sails carried away the maintopmast (just above the cap,) the foremast, and the bowsprit ; the part of the foremast below the deck afterwards shot right up, and floated away, leaving only the main-mast standing, and from the weight of wreck hanging to it, we expected that to go also.

We had now nothing but death to look forward to, as the tide was rising fast, and would inevitably in a short time sweep us off her side, where we were all collected to the number of twenty six, and only myself and one or two more free from dysentery. I expected so soon to be swept away, that I threw off my trousers and prepared for a swim, as I could see the land just on the horizon, and at any rate it was better to die endeavouring to save myself than to be drowned without making any exertion. Most providentially, the brig righted gra-dually, until the mast lay in an angle of about forty-five degrees, and enabled us to get, some in the maintop, (where we found a little dog belonging to the mate,) and others on the mainyard. As soon as we got aloft, we began cutting the sails away, as they held an immense quantity of water, and would most likely on that account cause the loss of the mast; we cut away the mainsail, trysail, and maintopsail, leaving only the masts and yards to hang on the mainmast, as with these we intended to make a raft.

The tide continued rising upon us, until half the top was under water, and hope was almost dead within us, when, to our inexpressible joy, we found the tide ceased to flow; no time was however to be lost, as in these places there is very little slack water, so we that could swim, immediately set to work, and collected all the spars and booms, masts and yards, we could, (for the rigging still held the topmast, &c.,) intending, when the tide had ebbed enough, to get on the wreck, which we expected would be almost dry at low water, and make a stout raft.   We could see some fishing-boats in the distance; but these, though they must have seen our disastrous situation, appeared to make no attempt to come to our assistance.

From so many being sick, and from the
Lascars refusing to assist us, we had very
few left to work, and before we had collected many spars, the ebb tide began to
run so strong, that we were obliged to leave
off, and take to the maintop again; the
spars we did get, we secured together, and
made fast in such a manner that the tide
could not carry them away. We now sat
down again on the top with hearts most
thankful that we had still a little hope left.
This was about four in the afternoon, and
in half an hour or so afterwards the jolly-
boat came in sight;* they had cleared her
of water, and they let go the grapnel just
abreast of ns. Mrs. Noble waved her handkerchief, but the tide was so strong that
they were driven past, completely out of
our sight, without being able to render us
the least assistance, or even being near
enough to speak to us. This was a most cruel
disappointment; but we had still our raft
to look forward to, and knowing that Mrs.
Noble and Lieut. Douglas were still alive

* Note 2.

was some consolation to us ; so we cheered one another in the best manner we could, relying upon Him who was able to save us from this apparently certain destruction.

By the time we could begin our work again, it was very dark, but we knew we should soon have a bright moon; so we set to work cheerfully, and had succeeded in collecting and lashing together a good many spars as a raft, when, to our great surprise, we found ourselves surrounded by Chinese boats, two of them large ones, and full of soldiers.

We all saw that resistance, if they attacked us, would be perfectly useless, and thought it would be better to trust to them than to the waves, so as they all seemed more intent upon plunder than upon us, Twizell and I, two or three of the marines. two of the first-class boys, and the greater part of the Lascars jumped into one boat, and the rest, with Webb and Wombwell, got into another. The Chinese wished us very much to get out again, but this we would not think of doing, as stopping by the vessel for another tide was quite impossible.

Finding that we were determined not to remain by the wreck, the Chinese gave in, and shoved off. To our great surprise, we had not gone a few yards when our junk was aground. The other boat made sail, and stood away. The men in our junk made signs for us to get out, when we again refused, fearing, if we did, they would leave us there; and not liking the idea of remaining on a sand which we knew the flood tide would cover. To have stopped by the wreck would have been pre.ferable to this.

We continued sitting in the boat, until one of the Chinese jumped out, and, taking his lantern, made signs to us to follow him; this we consented to do, and taking care not to let our guide get away from us, we went across the sand for about two miles, with the water sometimes above our knees, and sometimes only a little above our ankles. At last we arrived at another large boat, which was aground, and apparently waiting for the tide to float her. Our guide made signs for us to get into this boat, and that we should be taken ashore in her. This we did, and lay down to take a little rest, grateful that we had been enabled to save our lives, at least for the present.

We hoped that by some means or other we might reach Ningpo, where two English ships were cruising, and we knew that, if we could only once reach them, we were perfectly safe; but we had a very vague idea where we were, though we half suspected we were on the island of Ningpo; we afterwards found our suppositions to be correct.

It was now midnight, and when we left the wreck we could walk on her side, it being only six or eight inches below the surface.

CHAPTER II.

WE reached the shore about three in the morning, and the Chinese made signs to us, that if we would follow them, they would give us something to eat; we accordingly walked after them until we arrived at a small village, which consisted of a few miserable mud huts, with but one respectable brick house; but from these few huts a swarm of men, women, and children, poured out on our approach. We were taken into an outhouse, one half of which was occupied by an immense buffalo, and in the other half was a cane bed with musquito curtains; in one corner was a ladder, leading to a loft containing another

C

couch. They now brought us some hot rice, and a kind of preserved vegetable: we contented ourselves with the rice and a basin of tea, the preserve being so exceedingly nasty we could none of us eat it. Whilst in this place, a Chinese, who seemed the superior of the village, and doubtless was the owner of the one brick house, brought a piece of paper written upon in Chinese characters, and made signs for one of us to write upon it; intimating at the same time that he had written some account of us on this paper, and that he wanted an account in our writing, which I accordingly gave him, stating the time and cause of our shipwreck, and also our present situation; hoping that he would take it to the mandarin of the district, and that from him it might be forwarded to the authorities at Chusan, who might thus learn where we were, and take some steps for our return to the fleet.

When it was broad daylight we mentioned the name of Ningpo, and they made signs that if we would go with them they would show us the way there, so we started, as we imagined, for Ningpo.

Having no trousers, and my only clothing being a flannel shirt, and a black silk handkerchief round my head, which Twizell had given me when in the maintop, they gave me a piece of matting, but this proving rather an encumbrance than of any service, I soon threw it off, and walked on *sans culottes.*

We passed in this style through a highly cultivated country; on every side large plantations of cotton and rice, and various kinds of vegetables, but all unknown to me. Having gone six or seven miles, seeing very few houses, but crowds of people turning out of each as we passed, we at length arrived at a cross-road. Here another party of Chinese appeared, who absolutely forbade our proceeding any further: but as our guides went on, and beckoned us to follow, we pushed through our opponents and walked on; but they, having collected

c 2

more men, headed us, and we were obliged
to come to a stand-still. In this case we
found the want of a perfect understanding
amongst ourselves, for the Lascars were so
frightened at their situation, that they fell on
their knees before the Chinamen, which of
course encouraged the latter, and before we
could look around us, men rose up as it were
from the ground, separated us, and made us
all prisoners at once, with the exception of
four, who ran off, though without any idea
whither they should run, or what they
should do. Here the *Syrang made a foolish
attempt to cut his throat with a rusty old
knife he had about him, but he only succeeded in tearing his flesh a little, for he
was soon disarmed and pinioned. If, perhaps, we had all stood together, and put a
bold face on the matter, though without
any kind of arms, we might have gone
quietly to the mandarin's, and then have
been treated properly, but the conduct of
the Lascars emboldened our enemies, and
we were seized, bound, and dragged off,

* Note 3.

almost before we knew where we were. As
to those who ran away, they were obliged
to give themselves up after a short run,
and got a very severe beating, besides several
wounds from the spears the Chinese were
armed with.

From this time my narrative becomes
almost personal, as I can seldom give an
account of more than what befell myself.

When we were seized in the manner I
have related, a man threw his arms round
me, and though I could easily have shaken
him off, I saw five or six others gather-
ing round me, and I thought it would
be useless to struggle. It was better for
me that I made no resistance, as the
others were bound and dragged away,
with ropes round their necks ; whereas the
man who first seized me, still held me, and
walked me off, without binding me at all.
Twizell was amongst those that ran, and I
did not see him again till I got to Ningpo.
As I was walking along with my keeper,
we were met by two soldiers, who immedi-

ately stopped, and one, armed with a spear, prepared to make a lunge at me; but my old man stepped between us, and spoke to him, upon which he dropped his spear, and allowed us to pass.

At length we arrived at a large village, and here my first keeper left me, much to my regret, as, after he was gone, my hands, hitherto free, were made fast behind my back, and the cord being drawn as tight as possible, the flesh soon swelled and caused me great pain; another rope was put round my neck, by which they led me about.

At times I gave myself up for lost, but still I could not fancy the Chinese to be so cruel a people, as to murder us in cold blood, particularly after the manner in which we had fallen into their hands. I hardly knew what to think.

My new keeper led me into the court-yard of a house, and made me fast to one of several pillars that supported a rude kind of verandah, dragging the rope as tight as he could; however, he brought me some water

to drink, when I made signs for it. I had
not been here long, when one of the Melville's people was brought in, and made fast
to an opposite pillar; but we could not
speak to, and could hardly see each other, as
the yard was crowded with people anxious
to get a peep at us.

After standing here some time, a man
came and took me away to another house,
where, in the yard, was a quantity of cotton,
and in one corner, looking out of a window,
a Chinese gentleman and lady, before
whom my guide led me, and prostrated
himself, wishing me to do the same; but I
contented myself with bowing, upon which
the gentleman waved his hand, and I was
led to the back-yard, where my guide
brought me some rice and vegetables. I
did not feel so grateful for my dinner as I
perhaps ought, as I imagined this person
had bought me for a slave.

When I had finished my repast, I was
led back, and, being made fast to a tree, was
left exposed to the mercy of the mob, with-

out a guard. The people amused themselves with making signs; some, that my head would be cut off, others that I should not lose my head, but my eyes, tongue, nose, and all those little necessaries, and then be sent away—a most unenviable state to be reduced to. I was kept here some time, surrounded by a number of ugly old women, who seemed to take a delight in teasing me; but the most active of my tormentors was neither old nor ugly, being a tall and well-made person; her feet were not so mishapen as the generality of her countrywomen's; in fact, she was the handsomest woman I saw in China. At last a man came, loosed me from the tree, and led me off to a little distance; and while one man brought a stone block, another was sent away, as I imagined, for an axe, or some such instrument; before this block I was desired to kneel, but this I refused to do, determined not to give up my life in so quiet a manner as they seemed to propose. The messenger returned shortly, the block

Drawn by C. H. Greenhill.

Engraved by W. Lee.

was taken away, and I was led out of the village.

Being now guarded by a dozen armed men, I was led along the banks of a canal until I came to a bridge, where I saw some of my companions in misfortune; I could only exchange a hurried word or two as they dragged me past, as I supposed, to the place of execution. I went on thus, with two more of the prisoners at some distance before me, stopping now and then, and imagining every stoppage to be the last, and that I should here be made an end of; but they still led me on, until we came to another village, or rather town, and I was taken to what appeared to me to be the hall of justice. I was led to the back yard, and placed in a room, half filled with a heap of wood ashes. Here I found three more of the crew, in the same miserable condition as myself; but still, even here, we found some to feel for and relieve us a little, for, on making signs that my hands were bound too tight, one of the Chinese loosened the bonds, and afterwards went out : returning shortly with a lapful of cakes, he distributed them amongst us, and then procured us some water, of which we stood in great need, as we had had a long march under a broiling sun.

We had scarcely finished our cakes, when some of the soldiers came in, and took one of my fellow prisoners just outside the door ; as I could observe almost all that passed, it was with feelings of the most unpleasant nature that I saw him made to kneel, and directly surrounded by the soldiers ; one of whom came in, and took away a basket full of the ashes. I now supposed that we had in reality come to the last gasp; I fancied my companion's head was off, and that the ashes were taken out to serve in the place of saw-dust, to soak up his blood. I was not long kept in suspense, for the door opened, and some soldiers entered, who forced me to get up, and go out into the yard. I now took it for granted that my hour was really come ; but, to my great relief, they had only

brought me out to fetter me. They put
irons on my hands and feet, those on my
ankles being connected by a chain of five or
six links, and an iron collar round my neck,
with a stick fast to it, which was also made
fast by a padlock to my handcuffs. I hardly
knew whether to rejoice or not at this pro-
longation of my life, as I might be kept in
this condition a short time, only to suffer a
more lingering death in the end. When
my irons were on, and rivetted, I was led
into the outer yard, now crowded with
people, and again tied up to a post. On
looking around me, I saw my companion,
who had been led out before me, fastened
in a similar manner to the post opposite;
and in a short time they brought the other
two, and made them fast to the correspond-
ing corner pillars. We remained a short
time exposed to the insults of the lower
orders, who amused themselves with pulling
our hair, striking us with their pipes, spit-
ing in our faces, and annoying us in all
the petty ways they could think of. At

last our guards came, and led us to a small
room by the side of the gate, where we
again had some rice.

Here I saw a Chinaman prisoner, ironed
in exactly the same way as we were.

When we had finished our rice, we were
led through the town, down to the side of a
canal, where boats were waiting for us.
Into one of these they put me and a Lascar,
the other two prisoners in another boat,
each boat having a guard of several soldiers.
We were towed, by one man, so quickly
down the canal, that I had little time to notice the country, even had I been in a state
of mind to pay much attention. I could
see, however, that other canals branched
from ours in every direction, and on the
banks were an immense number of wheels
and machines of various descriptions, for
raising the water from the canals, and
irrigating the rice-fields; some worked by
men as at a tread-mill, and others by buf-
faloes, which walked round and round in a
circle, as we occasionally see horses in our

mills. By dusk, we arrived at a large town, where we had to change our boat; rather an awkward piece of business, as the guard would render us but little assistance, and, fettered as I was, I found it very difficult to crawl from one boat to the other. At last I managed it, and then lay down in the bottom of my new conveyance, the soldier taking the precaution of making my neck-rope fast, so that I could not escape.

About ten in the evening we arrived at another town, but, being late, everything here was perfectly quiet. I was now landed, and led through the town to the mandarin's house; on the way there, I tripped and fell, breaking the rivet of my fetters, and cutting my knee at the same time. The soldier who was leading me by the rope round my neck, said nothing, but waited very quietly till I had picked myself up again, and we proceeded on, till we came to the head mandarin's house.

Here, to my great joy, I found the greater part of those who had come ashore

in the junk with me; but still those who
had got into the other boat, on leaving the
wreck, and those who had run away, were
missing; and we could hardly hope ever to
see them again. I sat down on one of the
steps, an officer brought me some cakes,
and on seeing my knee, which had rather a
deep cut, brought a small bottle, from which
he sprinkled some kind of powder on the
wound: this immediately stopped the bleed-
ing, and in a day or two the part was
healed.

I sat here a short time, without being
allowed to speak to the others; till suddenly
we were made to stand up and place ourselves in two rows, and the mandarin and
two of his officers made their appearance.
They walked down the rows, stopping at each
person, and by signs asked if we had had
guns or opium on board our vessel. We
only shook our heads in answer to their
questions, and as we were not able to understand the other signs, they very soon
retired.

When they were gone, the soldiers led us across one or two yards, into a joshouse. By the light from the torches, I could distinguish, in a place railed off from the rest of the building, some people lying apparently asleep. At first I imagined them to be Chinese ; but to my amazement and great joy, I soon discovered this party to consist of Webb and Wombwell, and those who had left the wreck in the other junk, and of whose fate we had hitherto been in ignorance. In consequence of some misunderstanding, they had been most severely beaten by the Chinese, and from the effects of this beating two of the marines had died on their way from the coast to this town. Though dead when they arrived, the Chinese had, nevertheless, put irons on the bodies. The corporal of marines had been so ill treated, that he could not move without assistance; and in fact they had all experienced worse treatment than our party.

There were now missing only the four who had run off when the Chinese stopped us at the cross-way. Of Mrs. Noble, and those in the jolly-boat, we, of course, knew nothing ; but hoped that they might have escaped the Chinese, and managed to reach Chusan.

Having related our different stories, and consoled each other in the best way we could, we lay down on some loose straw for the night, and, notwithstanding our miserable condition, we slept soundly.

CHAPTER III.

In the morning, when I awoke, I found I was in a temple; outside the railing was a large hall; on each side, rows of seats were ranged, with a broad space in the centre; the sides of the building were quite plain, and so also was the roof. Inside the railing was a green silk canopy, under which were several images, handsomely dressed in different coloured silks. Standing against the walls were four more figures the size of life, one painted entirely black, another red, and the other two variegated; and all armed with some extraordinary instruments of warfare. These I suppose represented their gods, and were tolerably well done,

D

but not to be compared to others I afterwards saw. The whole building was so
destitute of any ornaments, that, had it not
been for the images, the idea of its being a
joshouse would not have struck me.

Breakfast was brought in early, consisting of sweet cakes and tea.   When we had
finished, two wooden cages were brought;
the Chinese lifted one of our men into each,
and carried them outside the gate, to be
looked at by the common people; whilst
the gentlemen, and better class, with their
families, were admitted about two dozen at
a time, to look at us who remained inside:
sometimes we were visited by a party consisting entirely of women; they were a
remarkably plain set, their pretensions to
beauty, in their own eyes, appearing to lie
in having the face painted red and white,
and the feet distorted into a hoof-like shape.
After keeping those in the cages outside for
about two hours, they were brought in, and
two fresh ones were taken out.   Those who
came in, told us that the bodies of our two

poor fellows, who had been killed the day before, were lying outside on the grass, with the fetters still on. Fortunately it soon began to rain heavily, when the other two were brought in, and the crowd gradually dispersed.

About noon we had our dinner; one basin full of rice and vegetables, and cakes and tea, as before ; our jailers would never give us plain water, but whenever we asked for anything to drink, brought us weak tea. For supper we had cakes and tea again, and, after this last meal, lay down on our straw for the night.

The next day was passed in a similar manner; towards evening there was a great mustering of cages in the hall; little did I think for what purpose they were intended. After the Chinese had ranged these horrible things in the open space in the centre, they made us all get into them, one into each. I forgot to say that before we were put into our cages, our jailers gave us each a loose jacket and a pair of trowsers, besides as many cakes as we could carry. In these wooden contrivances—which were not much unlike what I imagine Cardinal Balue's machines to have been, only ours were wooden and portable—we had neither room to stand, sit, nor lie, so that we were obliged to place ourselves in a dreadfully cramped position. Some few of the cages had a hole cut in the lid, large enough to allow the top of the head to pass out: into one of these I was fortunate enough to get; but those who were not so lucky, had the misery of sitting with their heads on one side, to add to their other discomforts. Afterwards I was put into one without a hole, and miserable was my position.

When we were all stowed in our separate cages, we were carried down to the side of the canal, and placed in boats, two cages in each boat, attended by a mandarin officer and several soldiers. My companion was a marine, one who had come ashore in the junk with Webb and Wombwell, and was still suffering from the effects

of his beating, besides being almost dead
with dysentery. We lay alongside the
quay till nearly midnight, the soldiers and
other people constantly running backwards
and forwards on shore, with torches and
gongs, shouting and making a great noise.
About midnight we shoved off, and started
down the canal; but as the junk was
covered over, and it was very dark, I could
see nothing of the country.

We soon appeared to be in a wider
stream, as they made sail on the boat, and
we went along at a rapid rate. In the
morning I found that we had got out of
the canal, and were in a river, going down
with wind and tide. At any other time I
should have enjoyed myself very much, but
at present my future prospects were too
far from agreeable to allow of anything approaching to enjoyment.

The banks of the river appeared to be
well cultivated; here and there some mili-
tary stations might be seen, distinguished
from the other houses by their flag-staffs.
Many junks were moored alongside the

bank, some very large, one in particular, whose long streamers flew gaily out in the breeze.

We stopped at a town on the left bank, where the soldiers got some firewood, and immediately set to work to prepare breakfast; rice, and some compounds of I know not what, for themselves, and sweet cakes and tea for me and my companion; but he was too ill to eat, and was constantly craving for water, which was never denied him. On our arrival at this town, the people crowded into our boat, nearly capsizing her; and to my surprise our guards made no attempt to keep them out, but on the contrary rather encouraged them. They had not long to satisfy their curiosity, for as soon as the soldiers had procured all they wanted, the boat was shoved off, and they hoisted the sail again. We continued our way down the stream till we arrived at another large town on the left bank. Here we stopped again, and I could soon see we were to be disembarked. The people crowded to see us as usual, but one of the soldiers, throwing part of the sail over the tops of our cages, kept watch over us, and would allow no one to molest us.

On the sail being removed, that we might be taken out of the boat, the first thing that met my eye was one of our guns, with the carriage belonging to it; soon after I saw another gun and its carriage. To enable the Chinese to get these guns, the tide must have fallen considerably after we left the wreck. The sight of these guns, as may be imagined, caused me anything but pleasurable sensations, as they proved beyond a doubt to our captors, that we had come to their coast with warlike intentions; and though they would perhaps be ashamed to kill a few shipwrecked merchant sailors, they might not hesitate to do so, if they could be certain that we had been concerned in the recent warfare, and these guns were strong evidence against us·

On being taken out of the boat, a long bamboo was passed between the bars of my cage, and two men, placing the ends on their shoulders, lifted it off the ground ; and in this manner I was carried through an immense crowd, the bearers sometimes stopping to rest, and placing my cage on the ground, upon which the people gathered round and began to torment me, as they had done in former cases. At length, after passing through a great many streets, some of them very gay, we arrived at an open space, at the end of which were large folding gates ; through these I passed, and after going up one or two passages, I found myself in a large hall. It was a large plain room, with a balustrade running down each side, behind which were several rough horses, saddled and bridled. At the end opposite the door was a large red silk canopy, under which was a small table, covered with a green cloth, and on it several metal plates and vases, dedicated to the manes of the ancestors of the person to whom the house belonged.* Many of the prisoners in their cages had arrived before me, and the rest followed in due time.

* Note 4.

The Chinese ranged us in our cages in two
lines, one on each side of the hall; and at
the end of each line they placed one of the
guns, with its muzzle towards us. When
we were thus arranged, like beasts in a
show, many well and richly-dressed people
came to look at us; and none but the
better sort seemed to be admitted, for, with
the exception of the soldiers, there were no
ragged people in the place. Our visitors
were mostly dressed in fine light silks,
beautifully worked with flowers and figures
of different descriptions. All of them had
fans, some of them prettily painted, and
others plain. One or two of the men had
enamelled watches, which they wore hanging to their girdles by a gold chain. We
were treated pretty well by them, as they
gave us fruit and cakes, and sent water to
those who asked for it.

We did not remain long in this hall, for
our bearers again made their appearance,
and mine, shouldering the cage, marched
off, and I was once more exposed to the

mercies of the mob; the soldiers, our guard, never making the slightest attempt to keep the people off. Fortunately for me I had had my hair cut close only a few days before we were wrecked, so that there was little or nothing to lay hold of; for the people on one side would pull my hair to make me look their way, and those on the other side would instantly pull again, to make me look round at them; and I, being ironed, hands, feet, and neck, could not offer the least resistance, but was obliged to sit very patiently, or, in other words, to grin and bear it.

Heartily glad was I when again taken up and walked off with. After passing through many streets, I arrived at a mandarin's house, and was placed with the other prisoners in a small court. Some empty cages were standing about, larger than the one I was in, and with small yellow flags flying on their tops.

In a short time some officers came in, and opening the lid of my cage, lifted me

Drawn by C. H. Greenhall

Engraved by W. Lee.

out, and led me out of this court into a larger one. To my great delight I here saw Twizell, and the three of the crew that had been missing, sitting in one corner, under a tree. I could not stop and speak to them, my guides hurrying me on. We scarcely recognized one another, so much were we altered.

I walked on for a short time, meditating on the past events, and wondering what my fate would be, when, raising my eyes from the ground, to my astonishment I perceived a man walking before me, heavily ironed, and whom I had never seen before. He was evidently an Englishman, and seemed almost in a worse condition than myself. When he heard me clanking after him, he turned round and spoke a few words, expressing his sorrow at seeing any one else in such a situation. I asked him who he was, and how he came there; but before he had time to answer, he was led down one passage, and I along another; so I could neither learn who he was, nor where or how he had been taken.

On emerging from the passage, I found myself in a small paved court, and in the presence of several mandarins. In the centre of this court an old Chinaman was kneeling, fettered as I was; there was no guard over him, and nobody seemed to take the least notice of him, at least not whilst I was there.

To my surprise, one of the mandarins addressed me in English; there was also an interpreter present, a native of Macao, and a prisoner like myself, having his legs in irons.* After they had asked me several questions concerning the Kite, where we had been, whither we were going, and how we were lost, I was sent away, and the other prisoners were brought up, and interrogated in the same manner. They asked all of us our names and ages, wrote our names on a strip of cotton, and sewed it to the backs of our jackets. We were then all sent away: the Chinese had brought all the cages from the outer to the inner yard, round which they had ranged them.

* Note 5.

I now had an opportunity of speaking to
Twizell and the others who had run away,
and was sorry to hear that two of them,
(marines) had received several spear wounds,
and that all four had been severely bam-
booed when taken. They had travelled by
land all the way from the coast, in the
cages, having been put into them the day
after we were all captured, and had been
two days sooner in their cages than our
party.

The corporal of marines, who was se-
riously ill of the dysentery, was lying on
his back in the bottom of his cage, whilst
his legs were raised up in the air, and his
heels resting on the upper ledge, the lid
being thrown back. He had entirely lost
his senses, and was evidently dying fast;
the maggots were crawling about him, and
the smell that came from him was dreadful.
Fettered as we were, we could afford him
no assistance, and the Chinese merely
looked at him, and then walked off, holding
their noses.

The strange Englishman at this moment came by, and seeing his horrible situation, spoke to the interpreter who was with him, and he to the Chinese; upon which two of them, though with great reluctance, lifted the marine into a clean cage, and placed him in an easier posture. The stranger now told us that he was an artillery officer, and had been taken some days before at Chusan; but he was hurried away before we could learn his name, or anything more from him.

It was now late in the afternoon, and dusk coming on, we were again put into our cages, and carried through the town, till we arrived at the jail. We were taken across a yard into a long room, which was divided into four parts, by gratings run across. In this miserable place we found eight more prisoners, (Lascars,) some of whom had been for two months in the same sort of cages that we were in.* We were placed in the small divisions, the coops being ranged round three sides of

* Note 6.

each compartment, the fourth side being
the entrance. A chain was passed through
each cage, and between our legs, over the
chain of our irons ; the two ends being
padlocked together, we were thus all fastened one to another, and also to our cages.
In this most uncomfortable manner we
passed the night.

During the night the corporal I have
mentioned died. He never recovered the
use of his senses.

In the morning the jailer came in, an old
man, with a loud voice, cross look, and a
piece of thyme, or some other herb, always
stuck on his upper lip. He opened the lids
of the cages of the eight Lascars, and took
the irons off their wrists, thus enabling
them to stand upright, and shake themselves ;
we had no such indulgence, but were kept
fast. At eight o'clock our breakfast was
brought in ; it was jail allowance, two small
basins full of rice, and one of vegetables :
the cages were opened, and the irons taken
off our hands, whilst we ate our scanty

meal, which we had no sooner finished than we were fastened down again. We remained in this state all day, and after our evening allowance, were again secured for the night.

A little before dark, the watch was set, and a large gong, at a short distance, was struck once; upon which a number of smaller gongs struck up, and when they had finished, a boy outside the room began to strike a piece of bamboo with a stick, which noise was continued without intermission the whole night. This horrid noise most effectually prevented my sleeping. The large gong was only struck when the time changed, striking first one, then two, and so on, till it struck five; thus regulating the watches of the night, which, in China, I imagine, is divided into five; at any rate I always found it so.

The following morning the jailer unlocked the lids of our cages, and took the irons off our hands; so that we were at liberty to stand upright, and stretch our limbs; which,

from our cramped position, much needed
this relaxation. The large place we were
in, was, as I have said before, divided into
four smaller apartments, three of which
were occupied by us in our cages ; whilst in
the fourth were some Chinese prisoners,
who lived in it by day, but slept in another
part of the jail. Outside was a covered passage, in which were several stoves ; and
here the greater part of the Chinese
prisoners cooked their rice and other vic-
tuals. They had all chains on their legs,
but were otherwise free; and they gave us
to understand that they were imprisoned
for smuggling opium, or for using it. Some
were of the better class, being well dressed,
and eating their meals with the mandarin
of the place.

Two of the commoner sort had lost
their tails,* and one was minus his nose,
which gave anything but a prepossessing
appearance to his countenance.

* Note 7.

E

CHAPTER IV.

TOWARDS the middle of the day, there was a commotion in the yard, and soon afterwards, the jailers and some other people came in, and I and two more, a marine and a boy, were carried out; after waiting a short time in the yard, our cages were again shouldered, and we were conveyed through the town to the residence of a mandarin, but not the same house we had been at two days before. We were taken into the entrance-hall, which had the usual canopy at the further end; being, I suppose, the " Hall of Ancestors." I was released from my cage directly it was set down, and found myself with the Eng-

lish prisoner I had previously seen. He
told me he was Captain Anstruther, and had
been kidnapped at Chusan ; that our heads
were in comparative security, but that perhaps we should have a long imprisonment,
as the Chinese would only consent to give
us up, if the English would evacuate Chusan ; but to this condition we could not
hope the commander-in-chief would accede.
However, he was, at the desire of the mandarins, going to write to Chusan to this
effect, and by this means our countrymen
would know where we were, and perhaps
be enabled to procure our release. Whilst
I was talking with him, I saw one of the
marines, who had been brought to the
mandarins with me, lying behind a sedan‾
on a grass-plot, and knowing that he had
the dysentery, I feared the poor fellow was
dead ; but Captain Anstruther said he had
desired him to be placed there, that he
might have the benefit of the sun ; he had
given him some cakes, and afterwards procured him a pair of trousers ; he also

caused a doctor to be sent to him ; in fact, he did everything that lay in his power to ameliorate our condition.

In a short time I was summoned before the mandarin, and found the same party assembled as before, with the interpreter in waiting. I expected to be questioned concerning the strength of the fleet and army at Chusan ; but, on the contrary, the mandarins contented themselves with asking me the most frivolous questions about myself, whether I was married, how old I was, if I had a father or mother, and such like inquiries. When this examination was over, Captain Austruther was brought in, and as he was a " great captain," was allowed to sit on the floor of the room, whilst we sat outside on the stones. A plate of cakes and a cup of tea were also handed to him. The mandarins could not be made to understand how Captain Austruther and our party, both having come from Chusan, should not know each other ; nor indeed would they believe me, when I said I had

never seen him until the day before.
They questioned and cross-questioned me,
but to no purpose, as I had never seen or
even heard of such a person till then.
They could not comprehend the meaning
of marines, till Captain Austruther ex-
plained it by calling them " sea soldiers,"
by which name the marines ever afterwards
went.

They made many inquiries about Captain
Noble, his wife and child, and showed that
they knew much concerning our vessel,
from the numerous spies they had at Chusan. After a few more such questions, I
was dismissed; and, being lifted into my
cage, was carried back to the jail, where I
had my supper, and was then locked up for
the night. At dark the usual serenade
commenced, which noise, with my uncomfortable position, drove all expectation of
sleep, at least by night, out of my head.

Soon after we had finished our breakfast
the next morning, some of the Chinese

prisoners began to play on musical instruments, in different parts of the yard, and
independent of each other. One of these
instruments was something like a mando-
line, and played in the same way; but it
was a most monotonous affair, with trifling
variety in the notes; and the song was as
bad, a kind of sing-song noise, with very
little pretensions to the name of music.
Another was a kind of small violin, played
with a bow; the player could only produce
a wretched noise. One man had a small
fife; he was not a whit superior to his fellows, though they seemed lost in rapture
at their own performance, and remained
strumming and blowing all day long,
barely allowing themselves time for their
meals.

The next morning, Wednesday, two more
of our party were taken to the mandarins,
and on their return reported the arrival of
Mrs. Noble, Lieut. Douglas, Mr. Witt, our
chief mate, and the two Lascar boys, who

had escaped in the jolly-boat. They told us that Mrs. Noble was in the same kind of cage that we were in. I could scarcely believe them, till the two Lascar boys were brought in, and they confirmed the statement. They had not only put her in a cage, but had also put irons on her, treating her in the same manner as they did the male prisoners; and, indeed, in some instances even worse. The mandarins had not the humanity to order her to be taken out of the cage, but let her remain there.

Soon after the boys had come in, Lieut. Douglas and Mr. Witt were brought into the jail, not to our place, but to the rooms on the other side of the yard; and though we could see them, we had no opportunity of speaking. They had been drifting about in the boat for three days, in great misery, not having had any food, except a little dry rice, and some water, out of a junk which they boarded; till at last, being obliged to go on shore, they were made prisoners. I had hoped they might have reached Chusan, and given an account of the loss of the Kite, and the probability of our being prisoners.

Next day, Saturday, Lieut. Douglas and Mr. Witt, who were kept on the opposite side to us, were taken out of their cages in the daytime, and allowed to walk about the yard; and as they were not prevented coming over to us, they heard our tale, and related theirs in return. Captain Austruther and Mrs. Noble were kept in separate rooms in another yard; they also were allowed their liberty by day, but when night came, all were locked down in their cages. Through Captain Austruther's entreaties (who had many opportunities of seeing the mandarins, besides having the advantage of the captured interpreter's company) a doctor came to see some of the prisoners, two of whom had the dysentery very badly, besides several who had spear wounds, and others whose flesh the irons had galled and worked into sores; to the latter he applied plasters, with a pink

powder, which healed them in a short
time ; but as for those who had the dysentery, he merely felt the pulse, looked at
them, and went away, leaving orders that
the lids of their cages should always be
left open, and the irons taken off their
hands,

On Monday morning, Lieut. Douglas
came over, and told us we were all going
to be removed to a more comfortable place ;
he and Mr. Witt very soon after were taken
away. We had an early supper, and as
soon as we had finished, some mandarin
officers arrived, one carrying a small board,
with some Chinese characters upon it.
Their arrival caused a great bustle, and the
jailer came in, unlocked the long chain
that went through all the cages, and took
five of the prisoners away with him. They
walked out of the yard, and soon after he
returned and took five more, and so on
till it came to my turn ; I was then lifted
out of the cage, and walked out of our yard
into a smaller one, where the ring was

taken off my neck, and the irons off my hands, my legs still remaining chained. I was here motioned to sit down on a small form, and on looking round I perceived Mrs. Noble standing at a gate in one corner. I had not seen her since the wreck, so wishing to speak to her, I got up, and was going towards her, but my keepers immediately stopped me, and one, to my surprise, said, " Must not, must not." I turned to him directly, and said, " Do you speak English?" he replied, " Yes, sare;" though on my asking him some other questions, he either would not or could not answer me. On my again attempting to go to Mrs. Noble, he repeated his former expression, and put his hand on my shoulder to prevent my rising. I was obliged, therefore, to content myself with exchanging a few signs with her.

I did not remain long in this place, for I was soon walked out into the open space before the prison, where I found some sedans, into one of which I stepped.

They were open in front, and the ends
of the bamboos were fastened together
by a crosspiece of the same material,
which the bearers, by stooping, placed on
their shoulders, and raising the sedan
from the ground, trotted off with us at a
great rate ; several soldiers going before to
clear the way.

Some of the streets through which I
passed were rather broad, and all were
paved with loose flags, not cemented together. The different trades appeared to
have their particular streets; the dyers
were in one part of the town, the braziers
in another, and so on : some of the shops
were very well set off, and all quite open to
the street. The houses were mostly built
of wood, and the names and occupations of
the owners were painted up and down the
door-posts, in yellow and other bright
colours, some being gilded, giving the
streets a gay appearance. Here and there
was an opening where a joshouse stood ;
the pillars and other parts of the front

gaudily painted and ornamented; and on the roof were placed several images. I passed several open doors, which led into courtyards belonging to apparently large houses; the courts were thronged with women and children, who all crowded to the entrance as I passed. Neither in this, nor in any other instance did they appear to be deprived of liberty, or to live secluded. The streets had generally a door at each end, in an archway; and this being shut at night, relieves the shopkeepers from the fear of thieves, to whom their open houses would otherwise be very easy of access. The butchers' shops were well fitted up with huge wooden slabs and blocks, and quarters of immensely fat pork hung up for sale; geese, ducks, vegetables, and fish, were all exposed in the broad open streets, as if in a market. I was carried across several bridges, which were built over black, slimy, sewer-looking places, from which, and from the streets themselves, arose even more than the two and seventy several stenches of Cologne.

My bearers trotted on through innumerable streets, the soldiers clearing the way before them, not a difficult task, as the curiosity of the inhabitants seemed satisfied, and there was little or no crowd, the people merely coming to their doors and looking at me as I passed. I arrived at length at the end of my journey, the sedan stopped, and I walked out; then turned to my left up a narrow courtyard, and at the end found several mandarins sitting with their officers. I ought to have said before that we knew the mandarins by the balls or buttons on the top of their caps, there being four kinds that I saw—red, blue, white, and crystal; red, I believe, being the highest rank. The officers were distinguished by gilded balls, having one o two tails of fur appending to them, according to their rank. I made a bow on passing, which they all returned; and I was led across a small yard, where I observed large earthen pans for catching water. I walked into a small square room, and

again joined the Englishmen who had preceded me. The floor was covered with
mats, and the change from our cages was
most agreeable. In a short time some
more of the prisoners arrived, and the
room was filled with eleven Europeans
and four Lascars, making fifteen in all,
just as many as the room would hold;
nine being on one side, and six on the
other, the rest of this side being occupied
by a water-bucket, and two small wash-
ing-tubs. It being now dark, we began
to think of sleep, so we lay down, which
there was just room enough to do, each
man lying on his back, and the feet of
both rows meeting in the centre; so that
we had little space to toss about in; however, this was paradise to the cages, and
thinking we should not remain here long,
we made ourselves as comfortable as cir-
cumstances would allow.

The next morning a servant brought us
some water to wash ourselves, (the first time
we had been allowed this luxury,) fine white

rice boiled in water, and served up in small wooden tubs. We had as much rice as we wished for, and a kind of stew, very much like old rags boiled, in one dish, and salt-fish in another; the dishes were of common earthenware, and shaped like a bowl. There being fifteen of us, we divided ourselves into three messes, five in each, and to each mess was brought a tub full of rice, one dish of stew, and one of very small fish, salted, and served up raw; but I could not make out what they were.

After this meal I began to look about me; the night previous having been too dark for me to notice any of the surrounding objects.

The room I was in, I found, was partitioned off from another, in which was a bed, with two or three chairs, and a small table. In this room lived an old officer, of some rank, I suppose, as all the soldiers, and our jailer, paid him great repect. Two young men came to him every day; whom we used to see, standing up before him, with their hands behind their backs, like schoolboys, saying their lessons to him. It looked, as ours did, into a small court, in which, also, were some of the same kind of large pans for catching rain water, as those before mentioned. Two sides of the apartment in which I was placed, were of wood, and the other two of white bricks ; but they were so thin, and so insecurely placed together, that it would have required little strength to shove them down. The floor was an inch thick in dirt, and the ceiling (which was a great height) covered with cobwebs. It was a place that we might have got out of with very little trouble ; but when out, we should not have known which way to turn, if escape had been our object, and our dress and looks would have betrayed us instantly. The consequence of such an attempt might have been fatal; so that they had us as safely confined in this insecure building, as when we were in the cages, fettered and chained to one another.

In front of our room was one appropriated to the use of one of the keepers. An

old man, hasty at times, when rather
fou, but who always behaved civilly, and
in general, very kindly towards us. To the
left of his dormitory was a passage that led
to the cook-house; and to the right, another
that led into a large yard, on each side of
which was a spacious apartment, where their
jos-ceremonies were performed. Outside
our door was a passage, and a staircase
that led to the upper story. The passage led down to another large yard, one
side of which was walled up, and on the
other was a large open room, containing
chairs, tables, and sleeping couches, with
cane bottoms; this seemed the guard-room,
as soldiers were always there, playing with
dice and dominoes; and their arms (match-
locks, and bows and arrows,) were scat-
tered about. Beyond this room was another passage, which led to the room
where the sixteen Lascars were confined; a
smaller and far less comfortable place than
ours.

What opportunities I had of seeing the

F

building caused me to conclude, that it was
a jos-house, and of spacious dimensions;
but I saw no images, nor any religious ceremonies performed.*

The day passed on, and supper time
came; this meal was the same as the morning's : after it was over, and the room swept,
an officer came in, and distributed rugs
amongst us; one rug between two. These
were a great improvement upon the mats,
being soft to lie upon during the hot weather,
and warm to cover ns, in case of our
remaining there the winter. At dark, the
watch was set, the same as down at the jail,
only here the noise was not so incessant;
and indeed the watchmen very often fell
asleep, and left us undisturbed a long time.

* Note 8.

CHAPTER V.

THE next morning one of the Melville's boys was taken ill of the dysentery ; the doctor came to see him, and prescribed some medicine, which came in the shape of a bitter brown mixture; it did him no good, for in a few days he grew so much worse, that he was removed down to the jail again, where, by-the-bye, the two marines who were ill had been left, as they were unable to bear the moving. Poor fellows! they felt very much being separated from their comrades, and left behind; but it was of no use complaining; they were obliged to submit. As for the boy* that was taken from us, (the same that I dragged out of the water, when we

* These *boys*, as they are called in the navy, were all above one and twenty.

were wrecked,) he left us, I might almost say, with a determination to die, so entirely did he despair; his forebodings were too true, as he died shortly after in the jail.

The window was besieged all day by well dressed persons, who came to see "the lions;" at first we only looked again, but getting bolder by degrees, we turned beggars, and from every fresh batch that came to the window, we requested something— either money, tobacco, or cakes, not being very particular : if they refused to give anything, we immediately slid the panels to, which most effectually prevented their seeing us, and the soldiers, our guard, very soon turned them out. Our grating was blockaded continually in this manner for more than a week, when the visitors ceased to come, and we were left in quietness.

Being in so crowded a state, and never allowed to go out of the room, on any pretence whatever, the air soon became very unwholesome ; and animals, the natural consequence of such a state of things, began

to show themselves, and, in spite of our ut-
most exertions, increased upon us; so that if
the warm weather, which was very favour-
able to them, should continue, we stood a fair
chance of being devoured alive. But our de-
plorable condition fortunately raised up another nation, which, though living upon the
same body, made desperate war upon the
other creatures, and by this means they kept
each other under. The principal employment
in the morning was to overhaul our clothes,
and kill all we could catch—a most disgust-
ing way of passing the time, but yet most
necessary; the rest of the day was spent
either in walking up and down the room,
spinning yarns, or sleeping.

After remaining in this place about a
fortnight, we were one evening surprised by
the appearance of the compradore, who
came to ask if we wished to send to Chusan
for anything, as he was going there. As I
knew nobody there, and felt sure that
Lieut. Douglas, who was as kind and atten-
tive to us as opportunity allowed, would

write, and acquaint the proper persons with our situation and wants, I did not write, neither did any of the others; he therefore went away, saying, that in about three weeks he hoped we should all be free; but he added, " Mandarin big rogue ;" however, this was far better news than I expected, and I looked forward to his return with pleasure and anxiety.

Time passed on pretty well after this, and things were going on as usual; those who had been ill of dysentery on board the ship were gradually getting better, fear having worked wonders; when, about a fortnight after the compradore's visit, we were roused one evening by a noise in the passage, whilst we were at supper. The board which had before attended us, again made its appearance, and as soon as we had finished our repast, all the white men were walked out of the room, and, after waiting a short time in the yard, sedans having been collected, we were placed in them, and carried to the chief mandarin's house. After passing through numerous streets, we arrived at a green plot railed in; against the railings were placed several small flags, some yellow and some red, but all having Chinese characters upon them. Passing through a gate, we came to a pair of large folding doors, on each fold of which was painted a gaudy figure, bearing a sword, and very much resembling the king of diamonds in our cards, only not half so good looking. On each side of this huge door was another smaller, through one of which we were taken, and here our sedans stopped, and we alighted. At the end of this new yard was a canopy of red and green silk as usual; we sat under this canopy until we were summoned before the mandarins. We were then led through a large place, which appeared intended for an ornamental garden, several rocks being placed here and there, round which the path wound; but I saw no flowers, and very few green things of any description.

The room in which the mandarins were

assembled, was rather a large chamber, open in front, as it was the hot season; several couches, and glazed arm-chairs, were arranged about the room ; four large paper lanterns were suspended from the ceiling, and as the evening drew in, they, and many more placed in other parts of the room, were lighted. One or two more mandarins arriving, there was a great deal of bowing, and salaaming, and tea-drinking, after which they proceeded to business.

The compradore now made his appearance, and produced several letters, which he handed to me to read: on opening them, I found that they came from Chusan, with various articles of clothing, and other comforts for Lieut. Douglas and Captain Anstruther, clothes of all sorts for Mrs. Noble, and a quantity for the child which was drowned ; but nothing whatever arrived for the crew; although Lieut. Douglas had written for necessary clothes for us, as well as for himself. I read the letters over to the compradore, making him understand,

as well as I could, the nature of the con-
tents, and he repeated them to the mandarins, whose official took them down in
Chinese. When we had finished reading
the letters, Mrs. Noble, Lieut. Douglas,
Capt. Anstruther, and the mate, were
brought in, and their letters given to them;
they were also permitted to open their stores.
We were now allowed to converse together
for a short time. Until now, I had not been
able to speak to Mrs. Noble since the wreck.
The mandarins soon called us up, and told
us, by the interpreter, that all was peace,
and that in six days we should be sent down
to Chusan ; but, after giving us this agree-
ble intelligence, they inquired if we had any
clothes for the cold weather, which would
soon come on. I immediately said, " If we
are going so soon to Chusan, we shall not
require any of your clothes." They sent
out, notwithstanding, and soon after a basket
was brought in, containing our future raiment,
which the mandarins distributed amongst
our party. They gave to each man a large

loose coat, and a pair of leggings, made of dungaree, and lined with cotton.

They were very warm, and well calculated to keep out the cold, but very clumsy and heavy : still they were not to be refused, and indeed had it not been for this kindness of the mandarins, we should have been exposed, almost naked, to the approaching inclement season. But this anxiety to provide us with clothing for the cold weather, made me doubt very much whether six days, or even six weeks, would find us on our way to Chusan. As it turned out, it was exactly sixteen weeks from that day before we were released.

After another consultation amongst the mandarins, we were all called up again, and the irons taken off our legs, beginning with Mrs. Noble. This was a great relief, as our legs were quite stiff with their long confinement, and in most cases the iron had worked into our flesh. Whilst they were being taken off, the compradore desired us to tell the Lascars, who had been left behind in the prison, that if they made no "bobheree," their irons would be taken off also.*

Being once more unfettered, we were again separated from Lieut. Douglas and his party, and led away to another room, the ceiling of which seemed very much inclined to come down on our heads. There was a table here, and a couch. I had no sooner taken my seat on the latter, than a well-dressed Chinese put writing materials before me, red paper, Indian ink, and a small brush. He made signs for me to write, salaaming low at the same time; I immediately complied with his request, and wrote a few lines for him. I had no sooner done this, and returned his brush, than he produced a handful of pice, and presented them to me; my finances being very low indeed, this donation was not to

* However, they did not take their irons off until just before our release. Indeed, they always made a marked difference between the white men and the men of colour, holding up the thumb to signify the former, and the little, finger, the latter. Note 9.

be rejected ; I therefore accepted them, and
found he had given me between fifty and
sixty pice, (about four pence in our money,)
—very good pay, I thought, for writing half
a dozen lines.

In this room refreshments were brought
for us; hard-boiled eggs, fowls and pork
cut into small pieces, and two sorts of
cakes, one being plain, with small seeds on
the top ; the other very like dumplings,
with minced pork inside. In fact, there
was as much as we could eat, and all was
good of the kind ; at any rate, we completely demolished the good things, and
then we returned to our sedans, and were
carried back to our rooms. Here we fonnd
the Lascars anxiously awaiting our return ;
we told them that the mandarins said we
were going to Chusan in six days, which
good news raised their spirits very much,
and they began to abuse the Chinese, espe-
cially the female part of the community,
for having imprisoned them at all. The
next day our jailer brought us shoes and

stockings of Chinese manufacture, and
made signs that the Lascars' clothes were
being made, and would very soon be
ready.

In the course of the same day, my friend
of the previous night came and requested
me to write something more for him; I of
course consented, and he then produced
some plain white fans; I wrote a few lines
upon them, and he seemed much pleased
with my performance; Wombwell also
wrote on one for him. In return, he gave
us two a basket full of sweet cakes, which
were very acceptable; he came to see us
several times afterwards, and never failed
to bring some token of his gratitude with
him.

Time wore away: the six days went by,
and we were not released; some said they
were perhaps waiting till the Lascars'
jackets were ready, but they were brought,
and we were still kept prisoners.

With the new clothes came also some of
those horrid creatures by which we had

been tormented; these coming fresh from
the tailors' hands, made us observe our
guards a little more closely, and we could
plainly discern that they were swarming
with vermin. We were glad to find
that what we had at first set down to our
own dirt and unwholesomeness, was more
attributable to the dirt and laziness of our
jailers and other people. Even the walls
had their inhabitants, for they fell down out
of the rafters upon us.

Days and weeks passed on, and we
gave up all hopes of a speedy release, expecting nothing less than an imprisonment
of a year or two; but I cannot say that I
was now much troubled with the fear of
losing my head. During this time we
were sometimes amused with a fight in the
yard, between two of the soldiers—a most
unpleasant kind of combat, for they seized
hold of each other's tails with one hand,
and dragging the head down almost to the
ground, clawed and scratched with the
other hand, till the one with the weakest

tail rolled over and gave in; we always tried to get out and see fair play, but the soldiers mustered too strong at these times. Sometimes, again, a drunken soldier would make his appearance, and coming to the window afford us a little amusement, for, getting hold of his tail, we made it fast to the grating, and then left him to get loose as he could; generally one of his comrades, attracted by his bellowing, came and released him; all this was not very edifying employment, but it served to pass the time, which, having no books or employment, hung very heavily on our hands.

The weather now changed, and the winter set in; we were glad to put on our thick clothes, which we found very comfortable, except that they afforded a great harbour to the vermin: this was, however, by this time only a secondary consideration, as the cold weather had rendered them very torpid, and they did not bite so hard. We had only two meals a day, morning and evening, and these being soon settled, and

not being allowed anything in the middle
of the day, we made bags of our old clothes,
and at breakfast-time filled them with
rice, when the servants were out of the
room, and stowed them away for a mid-day
meal. The servants discovered it once or
twice, but we generally managed to secrete
some rice from our breakfast.

The Chinese used now to carry about
little teapots, full of hot water, at the
spouts of which they were constantly sip-
ping; and also a kind of salamander, an
oblong brass vessel, with a handle to it, and
filled with hot water; in the lid were
several small holes, and the steam coming
through kept them warm. They carried
these things either in their long loose
sleeves, or, sitting down, placed their feet
upon them; but I should have imagined
that the steam would have damped their
clothes, and rather chilled than warmed
them. About this time, having got rather
free and easy with our jailers, one of our
party slipped out into the passage, whilst

the servants were removing the rice and
dishes, and brought in the piece of bamboo
and stick, which the watch used at night;
in the evening we saw the soldiers search-
ing for it, but we kept quiet till dark, and
then we began to keep watch ourselves;
but the noise soon brought our jailer in,
who took the bamboo away, threatening to
put us in irons. This threat made but
little impression, for, a short time after,
another of the party walked off with a tea-
pot belonging to one of the soldiers; this
we kept for several days, till the owner
found out where it was; but we would not
give it up unless he paid for it, and as our
jailer and his own comrades only laughed
at him, we obliged him to redeem his tea-
pot with a hundred or more pice, much to
his dissatisfaction.

G

CHAPTER VI.

ONE evening, about the latter end of
November, we were surprised by the appearance of the moving board, and expected that we were to be taken away
again, when, to our great amazement, one
of the marines that we had left in the
prison walked in, looking stout and well ;
but after him came, or rather was carried,
the other, a most horrid spectacle, a
moving skeleton, with the skin stretched
tightly over his bones ; his eyes were sunk
deep in his head, and his voice was awfully
hollow ; he was the most melancholy sight
I ever saw. When on board the ship he
was a stout, well-made man, and now how
dreadfully changed ! he had come up merely

to die with his old companions. The other
had been very ill indeed, but (owing to a
good constitution, and the kindness and
attentions of Mrs. Noble, who did all that
possibly lay in her power to alleviate their
sufferings) he had got over his sickness,
and was now in a fair way for recovery.*
They brought notes from Lieut. Douglas
and Mrs. Noble, promising us some money.
The marines had received their pice, and
ours were to come the next day, which they
accordingly did; four hundred pice for each
of the white men, and three hundred for
each of the Lascars.

I now began to learn a little of the language, and found out the names of several
things in the eating way; such as pork,
beef, and all sorts of cakes, and the cele-
brated bird's-nest soup, which, by-the-bye,
was uncommonly good; these things we
were enabled to buy with the money we
had received.

* These two marines had their irons on their legs when
they came to us.

This evening the doctor came and looked at the sick man, and shortly after his visit, one of the servants brought him a dose, which he took. That night this old servant was constantly at our window, with a lantern, to look at the sick person. Towards morning the marine became much worse, and lost his senses, and soon after he died. He was no sooner dead than the servant, who had been watching very narrowly at the window, came in, and rolling the body up in a long coat, and taking it by the arms, threw it on his back, and making signs for one of the Melville's boys to keep the legs off the ground, they walked off with him through the gate, and some way into the town, till they came to an open space, where there was a shed with some straw in it. Here he laid the body down, and covering it decently with the coat, made the boy understand that it would be buried that night.

There were now only two left of the seven marines who came on board of the Kite

from the Melville; and it was not long
before one of these was taken ill; he soon
became so bad, that he was obliged to be
moved out of our room, and we hoped he
might be taken down to the jail, where he
would have better attendance, and the advantage of Mrs. Noble's kindness. Our
jailer and attendants made signs to this
effect, but they moved him only to another
part of the joshouse. He had received
several spear-wounds when he was taken,
which had never properly healed; and
when attacked by the dysentery, these
wounds broke out afresh, and reduced him
to a dreadful state, and it was not long
before we heard of his death. There was
now only one marine left.

A short time after this, a new interpreter,
who had just arrived, as he said, from
Canton, came up to us; he brought us two
letters to read, one from Mrs. Noble, and
the other from Captain Austruther, to their
friends at Chusan, requesting to have some
clothes and other things sent to them.

This man told us it would most likely be peace, and that we should be released in a short time. We complained of the smallness of our room, and of our having nothing but rice to eat, and said we wished to have meat sometimes ; he agreed that it was a most uncomfortable place, and promised to speak to the mandarins, and get all things put to rights for us. He then left us, I cannot say with revived hopes' for we placed but little reliance on his assurances, being by this time fully aware of the deceitfulness of the Chinese. He told us, however, that either Captain Anstruther or Lieut. Douglas would come to see us in a few days.

On this point he did not deceive us ; for two or three days after his visit, Lieut. Douglas, to our great pleasure, walked in : he was very indignant at the treatment we had received, and at our being confined in such a miserable place, and said he would get it altered immediately. We learned from him, that though the mandarins

pressed the officers to write to their friends
at Chusan, and promised that the letters
should be safely conveyed, they had never
kept to their word, but had detained the
letters when they had obtained possession
of them; perhaps as curiosities. The officers at Chusan, finding that the prisoners
at Ningpo did not write, suspected the
cause to be something of this kind, and
therefore bribed a Chinese to carry letters
from them to Lieut. Douglas and the
others ; and they answered them by the same
person. They asked for all they wanted,
in their letters by the Chinaman, and
always mentioned the same things in those
that were given to the mandarins, so that
these gentlemen imagined the English were
conjurors, or some such thing ; for with all
their cunning they never found out the
spy, and the things that were written for,
through them, always came, although they
never sent the letters. Lieut. Douglas,
therefore, knew all that was passing at
Chusan, and could tell us what chance

there was of our being speedily released. He told us he had tried several times to get up to see us, but that the mandarins would not allow him to come. He had sent us several things, and amongst the rest a bar of soap; but none of these things arrived. I suppose the Chinese ate the soap; as they have no such article themselves, they would most likely imagine it to be some eatable; and as they are in the habit of eating far nastier things, the soap might have been rather a delicacy to them than otherwise. After some more conversation, he gave us a dollar apiece to procure us better and more substantial food, and then left us, promising to see us soon again, and to improve our situation.

Lieut. Douglas continued to supply us with money, at the rate of a dollar apiece for fourteen days; but the persons who brought it to us generally pocketed one or two dollars each time, and altogether robbed us of nine dollars; a large sum in that country, where the necessaries of life

are so cheap. The proper exchange, I
believe, is rather more than a thousand
pice to the dollar; but we could only get
nine hundred and thirty-two, or at most
nine hundred and fifty.

Christmas was now close at hand, and we
accordingly bought some meat and other
things, that we might not eat such an un-
Englishlike dinner as rice, turnips, and
very small fish, our usual food; and with a
little coaxing on our part, we prevailed on the
old jailer to allow us to have some samshu,
a liquor very like gin, and obtained from
rice. We made a better Christmas of it
than I had expected, and after our dinner
we called our jailer in, and drank his
health, to his great delight; in fact, he was
so much pleased, that he ran out of our
room, and immediately returned, bringing
with him a haunch of goat, which he said
" he gave to us;" and was going to hang
it up in our room, but we deemed it expe-
dient to place it in the outer air, so he
hung it up outside, and we had it for dinner

the next day. From this time we were
allowed to have as much samshu as we
liked; and with the exception of one Lascar getting drunk, no one ever forgot himself. The Lascar, when he came to his
senses in the morning, we tried by court-
martial, and sentenced him to receive three
dozen, which were administered with a cat
made for the purpose, of threads twisted
and plaited together.

The marine was now the only Englishman in irons, and notwithstanding the
mandarins had promised Lieut. Douglas,
in consequence of his remonstrances, that
they should be taken off, they had as usual
deceived him; so one day we took them off
ourselves, and lifting up one of the floor
planks in a corner of the room, hid them
there. This we were enabled to effect the
more easily, as they had been taken off
when he was at the jail, to allow him to
put on a pair of flushing trousers Lieut.
Douglas had given him; and therefore they
were not rivetted, but merely padlocked

together. The Chinese never noticed that his irons were off, and they were left in the hole as a legacy to the rats.

One evening, whilst at our supper, one of the soldiers came to the window, and amused himself by imitating our awkward attempts to eat with the chopsticks. This impertinence so incensed one of our men, that he jumped up, and filling a basin with water, dashed it through the bars into the soldier's face, taking him quite by surprise; the water streamed down his breast, inside his numerous jackets, and must have made him most uncomfortable. But his only revenge was swearing and shaking his fist at us as he ran away. Finding that no harm arose from this first attempt, we determined never to be annoyed again, regretting that we had allowed ourselves to be overlooked so long; therefore all parties that would not pay for peeping, we drove away by throwing water at them; and having a bucketful in the room, the water was always at hand. Our proceedings amused the old jailer exceedingly, and he very often brought people to see us, and then getting behind them, made signs for us to throw the water in their faces; taking care, however, always to get out of reach of the shower, and to condole with the visitors, who generally received a good ducking.

It was now January, and we had some very cold weather, and several falls of snow; our jailer, therefore, allowed us sometimes to have a small earthenware pot, in which was some mould, and on the top a few pieces of charcoal; this, of course, was soon expended, so, to keep up the fire, we tore out the bars of the door, and part of the flooring, and burnt them. These were the only things I saw in use at the joshouse in lieu of fire-places.

Our room was too crowded for us to feel the cold much, but still it was rather chilly; so, to keep ourselves warm, we ran round and round our apartment, played at leap-frog, and such other games, which kept the

blood from freezing in our veins; besides,
we bought pipes and tobacco, and constantly
smoked, which warmed us a little, and pro-
bably prevented sickness getting in amongst
us; this was a great advantage, for if any
fever had broken out, we might all have been
carried off, from the extreme unwholesomeness of our apartment. We could see the
old officer, who lived in the room next ours,
sitting, for hours together, in his yard,
basking in the sun, and smoking a long
pipe; wrapped up in two or three dresses,
made of skins sown together, and wearing a
curious kind of head-dress, resembling the
cap worn by jesters in the olden time, only
minus the bells.

Soon after Lieut. Douglas's visit, Wombwell and I were sent for by the mandarins;
thanks to the person for whom we had
written on the fans, as he came with the
servants, and pointed us out. On arriving
at the mandarin's, we found the Canton
interpreter, with several letters and boxes
from Chusan. The letters contained the

good news that peace was concluded; this
information, coming from English authority,
was the more likely to be true, and of course
gave me greater pleasure. The interpreter
wished me to explain the letters, which I
did, making him understand our expres-
sions as well as I could; I then told him to
whom the boxes belonged. Wombwell and
I were kept separate, and, after interpreting
one letter, I was sent away, and Wombwell
brought in, to give his interpretation. This
way of proceeding of course took a long
time; so that we were there nearly all day.
About noon a small table was brought in,
upon which they placed refreshments for
us; cold meat cut into small pieces, hard
boiled eggs, cakes, and a metal jug, containing about a quart of samshu. This
came in very happily, and the interpreting
went on with fresh vigour.

Once, when I retired whilst Wombwell
was giving his version of a letter, I was
taken to an officer's rooms, and saw him and
three others at dinner; but, notwithstand-

ing my signs to that purpose, they would
not allow me to share it with them. In the
centre of the table was a large bowl, with a
heater in the middle of it, containing a rich
soup, full of vegetables and meat, cut into
very small pieces. Around this were several large plates, containing pork and fowls
cut up, the bones having been taken out,
pickled fish and vegetables in a rich thick
gravy; two small plates, one containing
salted shrimps, and the other, something
exactly like sea-weed, and also a small
basin, filled with a white lard, into which
the officers dipped their chopsticks, and
taking out a small quantity, mixed it
with their rice. The rice, which was very
fine and white, was in a small wooden
bucket; from which the servants gave their
masters a fresh supply, when their basins
were empty. The chopsticks were made of
a hard black polished wood, something like
ebony; and the basins and plates were of
that beautiful transparent China ware
which we esteem so highly, with figures

and flowers painted on them, in most brilliant colours. Two servants stood behind their masters' chairs, and waited upon them with the assiduity of European servants. When the officers had finished, the servants took their places, and made their dinner off the remains. They followed their masters' example in excluding me from their repast; though they very readily gave me cups ef hot water, which I suppose they called tea, as I could discern two or three leaves at the bottom of the cup.

Having now nothing to do, I went to the entrance, and, on looking out, I observed, opposite to me, a building, from which proceeded a Babel of voices, and seeing a little girl come out of the door, I thought I would take the opportunity, whilst the officers were in another apartment, and the servants intent upon their supper, to walk over, and see what was in this place; so on the girl's return, I followed her; but was noticed too soon by the ladies inside, who no sooner saw me than they jumped up, and slammed the

door in my face, setting up most dreadful
shrieks, which brought the officers out, who
immediately ran over to me, and led me
back, laughing heartily at the same time;
so that my attempt to see a Chinese lady's
apartment was frustrated.

I now returned to the interpreter, and
having finished our task, the small table was
again placed before us, furnished in the
same manner as before; so that we could
not complain of their want of hospitality.

The mandarin, a fat jolly-looking old
gentleman, asked me, through the interpreter, whether we ever had any snow in
our country; and seemed very much surprised when I told him, we had far more
than was then on the ground; he was very
much taken with the appearance of my
blue flannel shirt, which I was then wearing: but as it was my warmest piece of
clothing, I could not afford to make him a
present of it. The room we were in was
very nicely furnished; with painted arm-
chairs, a few couches, with soft cushions,

H

small tables, inlaid with different kinds of woods, several handsome China vases, and a small English clock in a wooden case, inlaid with brass. The ceiling was painted buff colour, and varnished; and from it were suspended four large ornamented lanterns. There were neither rushes nor mats on the floor, but merely the bare boards, and these by no means too clean.

When we reached home, (as we were obliged to call our miserable prison,) it was quite dark, and we found all the others had lain down. We communicated the happy news we had learned from the letters, and then followed their example.

CHAPTER VII.

A NIGHT or two after our visit to the mandarin, we heard the priests chaunting, two or three silvery toned bells were struck at the same time, and now and then a drum. We could see nothing of their proceedings, but from the glare of light the temple must have been brilliantly illuminated. The priests were not exactly sober all the next day; so they must have taken strong stimulants during the night.

A few days after was the Chinese New Year's Day; when an immense number of worshippers visited the joshouse with offerings of various kinds; mostly ornaments of filigree paper. All the visitors were ex-

H 2

tremely well dressed; silks, satins, and furs of all descriptions, and very handsome dresses they were.

One of them, a man, arrayed in a splendid silk garment, had some words with our jailer, and I believe struck him, at least I saw his hand up: he was seized by the soldiers, and dragged by his tail to an inner court, from whence he was shortly led by a soldier with a long heavy chain round his neck, and handcuffed. What became of him afterwards I did not learn; but it seemed to me summary justice, and very hard usage, for apparently so slight an offence. The old officer, who lived behind our prison, wore a magnificent dress, something similar to a tartan, but the colours more varied, and brilliant. On his breast was a piece of beautiful embroidery; representing some extraordinary animal, only existing, I should suppose, in the imaginations of the Chinese. At his appearance, all the soldiers, and our old jailer, went to him, and made their obeisance; salaaming down to the ground; he returned it most graciously, and they then retired. In the evening rockets and other fireworks were going off in every direction. This festival was a great nuisance to us, as the generality of the shops were shut up for a fortnight, and we could only procure plain cakes.

It was about this time that Mrs. Noble sent us a New Testament, and Flavel on Providence, which were very acceptable indeed; and they enabled us to pass our time in somewhat more respectable a manner than heretofore.

We were sometimes very much amused by seeing our jailer's head shaved, and him in a manner shampooed, the operations altogether occupying a considerable space of time. The shampooing consisted merely of having the back well drubbed (for I can call it by no other name) by the barber, using one hand open and the other clenched; this was a finishing touch, after shaving him, and washing his head and face; the razors were excessively clumsy in appearance, but were very keen, and did their duty well.

Soon after the New Year's Festival, Wombwell and I were again sent for by the mandarins, and found letters to the same purport as before ; but in one of the letters was a Latin quotation, which led me to suppose that peace was not quite so close at hand as the English part of the letter gave us to understand ; however, this I did not translate, nor did I say anything about it to the other prisoners, thinking it was intended for the officers' private information. With the letters came some packets of medicine ; and amongst them several doses of Epsom salts, which the Chinese mistook for saltpetre, and were quite astonished that it did not take fire when they applied a candle to it. Seeing them so inquisitive, I tried very hard to persuade them to take some blue pills which had been sent, telling them that they were sweetmeats of some sort, and very good for the stomach ; but to no purpose, they were not to be taken in. This was a

thoughtless action, I must own, as the con-
sequences of the experiment, had I succeeded
in persuading them to take some, might have
made them imagine that we wished to poison
them. We then returned to our sedans,
and were taken home.

Just outside the gates of the mandarin's
house, I observed a number of people collected, and amongst them, several children
fancifully dressed, and crowned with artificial
flowers; I could not imagine why they
were arrayed in this style, unless they
formed part of some procession in honour of
the New Year.

During our absence, the jailer had been to
the window, making signs that we were all
going away; he appeared very much grieved,
and putting his hand to his breast, with tears
in his eyes, seemed to express his great
regret at having to part with us. At last,
his feelings completely got the better of
him, and he was obliged to run into his
room; where he shut himself up for the
remainder of the day; sending us, however,

some substantial marks of his regard, in the shape of stewed beef, bird's-nest soup, and samshu.

During the winter months, the Chinese amused themselves with kite-flying; their kites had a hole in the centre, across which were placed several strings ; and when they were up in the air, the wind passing through the hole produced a loud humming noise.   I suppose this was on the same principle as the Æolian harp. Some of them were very pretty and ingenious, being in the shape of birds and butterflies, the wings of which were made of loose thin paper, which fluttered about as they rose into the air.

Time passed, and we two paid several more visits to the mandarins, when we always heard the same reports of liberty.   I rather liked these visits, as they gave me opportunities which I should not otherwise have had of seeing a little of the Chinese ; besides the great advantage of getting fresh air, and being able to stretch my limbs.

On my last visit to the mandarin's, I saw

Drawn by C.H.Greenhill.

Engraved by W.Lee.

another coming in state to see him; and as
his attendants made rather a curious group, I
shall give a description of them. In front
walked two men, with high felt caps, to
which were appended two goose-quills,
having very much the appearance of a
large ink-bottle, with two pens in it; they
dragged chains after them; then came
two more, with the same curious head-
dresses, beating gongs; then a soldier,
with a red silk chatty, which he carried as
if about to charge; after him were two
more soldiers, and then the mandarin's
sedan made its appearance, carried by four
men, and surrounded by soldiers and other
attendants; the whole party were shouting, and making a great noise. When
they had passed through the great gate,
the train filed off to the right and left, and
the mandarin walked out of his sedan,
and went in; attended only by his pipe-
bearer, and one or two more officers. All,
with the exception of his immediate attendants, were *very raggedly clothed, and*

the sedan-bearers were almost naked, not-withstanding the inclemency of the weather; indeed, the *quantity*, and not the *quality*, of the attendants, seemed the order of the day.

I was rather struck with the manner of visiting amongst the Chinese, as showing a greater degree of refinement existing amongst them than I had any idea of. The person calling sent in his card, (a piece of red paper, with a few characters upon it,) and if the master of the house were in, or chose to see him, he went to the door, and took the visitor into the sitting-room, where tea was immediately served up. On the visitor's departure, the master generally accompanies him a certain distance, according to his rank; if a superior, to the gate; if an equal, or inferior, not so far: at the same time there being always a lengthened *combat de politesse* about taking precedence, although regular rules are laid down for their guidance on the subject, and they well know that after a certain number of bows, the superior must always go first.

During the month of February, the soldiers were constantly making signs, intimating that we were on the point of departure ; and some of them went away, carrying all their few worldly goods with them, so that we began to think our liberation was really close at hand.

One morning very early, before we had risen, a little boy, one of our attendants, came to the window, and shoving back the shutters, desired us to get up, for we were all going away ; but as we did not believe him, the only answer he received was a volley of shoes from all parts of the room, which quickly drove him away ; but soon after our old jailer came, and made signs to the same effect, and that our rice was coming in directly ; we therefore arose, still hardly daring to believe him. When breakfast was finished, the old man came in and told us to pack up our rugs ; that we were going away, and were to take

them with us. We then imagined Lieut.
Douglas's remonstrances had had some effect, and that, instead of being released, we
were only going to a more commodious
prison; however, even this was good news,
and we proceeded very joyfully to pack up
our little all. Outside the place was all in
confusion; a number of fresh soldiers made
their appearance, whilst our own guards
were taking their departure, (with their
beds and other traps.) The jailer was dis-
tributing his goods amongst the servants,
giving a pipe to one, a gown to another,
and so on. A number of coolies now came
in, and carried away our rugs. Our New
Testament we gave to the old jailer, who,
though cross at times, had on the whole
treated us very kindly, and with great consideration. Flavel we gave to an officer
who had often done us various good
offices.

In a short time we ourselves walked out,
and found in the passage a number of
sedans, in which we took our seats, one in

each, and they started with us. Thus, on the 21st of February, 1841, we left the place where we had been confined about five months.

CHAPTER VIII.

On getting outside the gate, we found an immense crowd assembled; they did not molest us in the least, but we passed on very quietly. We were taken through a different quarter of the town to any I had been in before, but the streets were built and ornamented in the same manner; they were lined, on both sides, with such a number of people, that where they could all have come from I could not imagine. We went on thus till we came to the gates of the city, where the mandarins were assembled to see us pass out. The walls were about eighteen feet thick, and twenty-five feet high; but the materials (stones and bricks) seemed so loosely put together, that a swivel might very soon have made a breach in them.

We were now in the suburbs, and close to the river, to which we were taken; and each sedan being placed in a separate boat, we were soon ferried across. The river here was divided into two branches, across one of which we had just been carried; and we went down the left bank of the other; it was about the breadth of the Thames at Westminster. As they conveyed me over, I got out of the sedan, and looked back at the place of my imprisonment. It seemed a large town, walled all round; but in some places the walls were n a very ruinous condition. On the ramparts and plain, outside the city, were thousands and thousands of people.

We were carried down by the water-side, still in our sedans; and as it was a cold day, and there was a good stiff breeze right in our faces, I got out of the sedan, and walked between the poles. I observed that I was not the only one, for I saw that all the white men were walking also; the Lascars, having their legs still chained, were unable to walk. The people in the villages turned out, everywhere in great numbers, to stare at us.

The crops were in some places beginning to make their appearance, and almost every inch of ground was cultivated; all that appeared bad unprofitable land was covered with tombs, and particularly the sides of the hills; in summer, the white tombs peeping out from the high grass and shrubs would have a very picturesque effect. The coffins were placed on the ground, and some were covered over with bamboo and matting; a very slight defence, which in many instances had given way, and left parts of the coffins exposed; other graves had square tombs over them, built of brick, and covered with a slab of red stone; but in some of these the bricks had given way, and the slab falling in on the coffin, had burst it open: others being, I suppose, for the superior class, were built entirely of stone, curiously and rather tastefully ornamented. The coffins being made of slight materials, the smell on passing the burial places was very unpleasant.

We continued our journey, sometimes walking, sometimes in the sedan, the officers scarcely ever allowing the bearers to rest, and indeed beating them severely with sticks, and their heavy sheathed swords, if they stopped for even a moment without leave. The old jailer was with us, in a sedan, and seeing us walking, he spoke to the officer commanding the party, who came and made signs for us to get into the sedans; but it was far too cold for an open carriage, and besides, after so long a confinement, the walk was agreeable. About dusk we came to the gate of another city, walled round in the same manner as Ningpo. We passed through several streets till we came to a large joshouse, before which a number of people were assembled. We went into the outer

I

court, and perceived, by the sedans, that
many mandarins and other officers were
within.   Passing through a building in
which were four colossal figures, about
twenty feet high, and painted in Chinese
style, we came to another yard, out of
which Mrs. Noble and Mr. Witt were
taken in sedans just as we entered.   I
heard them speaking, but they went past
so quickly, that by the time I had jumped
out of my sedan, they were gone.   I saw
Lieut. Douglas and Captain Anstruther,
who told me that we were all to be released
immediately, aud that Mrs. Noble and Mr.
Witt had already started for Chusan, whither we were to follow as soon as possible.

The interpreter then made his appearance, and desired me to follow him; this I
did, and soon found myself in the grand
hall of the temple, in the presence of a
number of mandarins and other officers.
The other prisoners were here; and another
interpreter, whom I had never seen before,

came round and asked our names and
country; he could also speak Bengalee,
and therefore interpreted for the Lascars.
They then took the irons off the Lascars'
legs, and after the mandarins had looked
at us for a short time, they took their departure, leaving us, with a few officers, in
the temple. I now had time to look about,
and found I was in a large hall, in the
centre of which were three colossal figures,
gilded all over, very much resembling
in appearance the Hindostanee idols; under them was a smaller figure of a
woman, painted in gaudy colours, and on
each side of her a small model of a temple.
Round the hall were other images, placed
in niches, and amongst them I particularly
noticed one of a woman, with a glory
round her head, and holding a child in her
arms, bearing altogether a strong resem-
blance to the virgin and child; two others
sat side by side, of rather singular appearance, one having a black face and hands,

with a white dress, and the other a white face and hands, and a black dress.

Several torches were placed in different parts of the wall, and the flickering light from these, glancing over the gilded images and the rich dresses of the officers, contrasted with our miserable appearance, produced rather a singular scene. We did not remain here long, for we soon had to return to our sedans, and were carried to the head mandarin's house, to wait till a junk was ready for us. On the way to his residence, I came to an open space, and before me could see a number of small lights dancing about. I imagined this to be the river, and the lights to be in boats, particularly as there was a curious noise exactly like an immense number of ducks feeding ; but, on approaching nearer, I found myself in a camp, pitched on a large plain. I was carried between two long rows of small tents, and before every other tent was a sentinel, with a piece of bamboo in one hand, and a stick in the other, with which he incessantly struck the bamboo, and thereby caused the clacking noise which had deceived me. Before every tenth tent another sentinel was stationed with a gong, which he struck at intervals; they were keeping the first watch of the night, which was about eight o'clock of our time. Having passed through the camp, we came to the mandarin's house, and were conducted into a court, where we found Lieut. Douglas and Captain Anstruther. A piazza ran round this court, and under it we sat, having the pleasure of seeing the mandarin's supper taken in, but none was brought for us, and we had had nothing to eat since the morning.

Through Lieut. Douglas's remonstrances, a few cakes and some hard-boiled eggs were at length presented to us; and Lieut. Douglas, going to one of his boxes, brought out two bottles of rum, which were very acceptable, and helped to pass away the time till twelve o'clock, at which hour we left the house.

Lieut. Douglas here told me that several plans had been arranged for our escape from Ningpo, but, from the known treachery of the Chinese, they had been dropped. Others also, for the escape of Mrs. Noble and the officers had been concerted, and Mrs. Noble's jailer had even been bribed to connive at the plan; but they most generously refused to go, and leave us to the mercy of the Chinese. He also told me he had many times tried to come to us again, but that the mandarins would never allow him; they assured him, however, that our condition was materially improved, that we had three or four hours' liberty every day, better food, and a more comfortable apartment, all of which was false. The unfortunate captive compradore the mandarins refused to give up at this time, but said they would send him down to Canton, to be given up there.

The mandarin (whom I understood to be commissioner E.) having by this time finished his supper, came to have a look at

us. He desired the interpreter to tell us
" that he was very good to us, and was
sending us away before the time; that he
himself was going to leave the island, and
another mandarin, the emperor's cousin,
was coming in his place; that if he arrived
before our departure, he would most pro-
bably keep us, and not let us go at all:
at the same time he desired Lieut. Douglas
to tell the commanding officer at Chusan,
to withdraw his men and ships as soon as
we were given up to them; also that a
great many soldiers would march into
Chusan as soon as our fleet left." We then
walked out, about midnight, to go to the
junk; on our way down, we passed through
two long files of soldiers, drawn up on
each side of the road, most unmilitary looking warriors; their only uniform was a
loose jacket, with some Chinese characters
inscribed on the back and front; the rest
of their dress seemed left to their own
taste, and a motley group they were. They
appeared to be divided into three bands,

one bearing long unwieldy spears, another bows and arrows, and the third having a sword in, each hand; these, the interpreter told us, were to embark the next day for Chusan. At the end of each file of soldiers a huge gun was placed, of immense thickness, but small calibre, not carrying, I should think, more than a twenty-four pound shot, if so much.

When we arrived at the water's edge, we found a sampan, or small boat, waiting; the Lascars and most of the Europeans having preceded us, Lieut. Douglas, Captain Anstruther, myself, and the others, got into the sampan, and were soon sculled alongside a junk, which the interpreter, who was with us, told us was only waiting for high water (which would be about three o'clock A. M.) to get under weigh. Mrs. Noble, and Mr. Witt, our chief mate, who had preceded us, were in one junk; the Lascars, who had also reached the water before us, were in another; and our party, Lieut. Douglas, Captain Anstruther, and

the Europeans, got aboard of the third.
Here we found our rugs, and after partak-
ing of some slight refreshment, in the
shape of hot water and sweet cakes, we
lay down to sleep. About three o'clock
the junk was got under weigh, and when I
got up in the morning I found that we
were out of the river, and sailing between
some islands, and the interpreter told us we
should soon be at Chusan.

The vessel was covered over with tilts,
made of split bamboo, leaving only the
forecastle and poop exposed; under the
forecastle-deck was the tank, and on deck
was a sampan, which could be launched
at will. The poop was a very small
place, there being only room enough to
work the tiller; and when the wind was
adverse, the long tiller was unshipped, and
a short one used instead, and the vessel
propelled by means of a large sweep,
which five or six men handled, sculling in
the same manner as we do. The sails were
made of cotton, with an immense number

of bowlines, and the tilts were sufficiently strong to allow the men to walk upon them, and stow or set the mainsail.

Under the covering were three divisions, or holds, in the foremost of which the soldiers, our guard, and the crew were; in the middle one a number of boxes (the cargo, I presume) were stowed, and in the third we ten Europeans were. Abaft this was the cabin, which Captain Anstruther, Lieut. Douglas, the interpreter, a mandarin, and the captain of the vessel occupied.

Breakfast was set before us about eight o'clock, consisting of rice, very white, and well boiled, pig's cheek in small pieces, eggs, preserved, I think, in lard, as they were very greasy, pickled fish, and various other things; had I not been able to distinguish the mark of division between the yolk and white of the eggs, I should not have discovered what they were, as they certainly had neither the taste nor appearance of eggs, being of a deep chocolate colour;

however, they, and all the other things,
were very good, and we made an excellent
breakfast.

The Chinese now pointed out where-
abouts Chusan lay, and we saw, over a
point of land, the masts of some English
vessels. About ten o'clock we rounded the
point, and got into the bay, where several
men-of-war and transports were lying; we
soon were abreast of them, and a boat from
one of the men-of-war came alongside,
and finding that we were on board, made
a signal to their vessel, when the lower
rigging was manned, and they gave us
three cheers; on seeing this, the other men-
of-war and transports did the same, and the
bands on board the transports struck up
" Rule Britannia." What my feelings were
at the moment may more easily be imagined than described; after five months'
imprisonment I was once more free, and
in the hands of my own countrymen. I
was penniless, and I might also say naked,
for I knew that the clothes I had on would

have to be thrown away; but I was going amongst Englishmen, and at that time no anxiety for the future troubled me.

We Europeans were taken on board of H. M. S. Blonde, Captain Bourchier, where we were rejoiced to meet Mrs. Noble again, and congratulate each other on our liberation.   Mrs. Noble the same day left us, and went on board a transport: I went to see her again at Macao, where she remained.   Lieut. Douglas and Mr. Witt remained on board the Blonde, Captain Anstruther went to a transport, and joined his regiment, and the Lascars were sent on board another transport.

The next day we left Chusan, and arrived in a few days at the entrance of the Canton river, where H. M. S. Columbine informed us that hostilities had again commenced, and that the forts at the Bogue had been taken a week before.

A short time afterwards we heard that, two days after our release from Ningpo, an order had arrived there from the emperor of China, that all the prisoners were to be sent to Pekin, to be publicly exhibited, and then put to death, by being cut into a thousand pieces.

Report also said that Commissioner E., who had rather hurried our departure, had been sent in irons to the capital for having released us.

The Blonde proceeded up to Whampoa, and I was on board of her altogether a month, when, at our request, we were sent down to Macao in the Hebe tender, where we saw Captain Elliot, the Plenipotentiary, and Lieut. Douglas. They procured a passage for Twizell, Webb, Wombwell, and myself to England, in H. M. S. Samarang, Captain Scott; but afterwards, Twizell having gone ashore to buy some clothes for us, the ship got under weigh, and he was left behind.

We left Macao on the 29th March, 1841, and having touched at the Mauritius, St. Helena, and Ascension, anchored at Spithead on Monday, the 10th August. On

Wednesday we left the ship, and proceeded to London.

To Lieut. Douglas and Captain Anstruther I shall ever feel most grateful for their kindness towards us, and their unceasing endeavours to ameliorate the miserable condition of their fellow-prisoners at Ningpo.

NOTES.

Note 1, *Page* 8.

Lord Jocelyn, in his " Campaign in China," gives a very erroneous account of the loss of the Kite, but as he obtained his information from some mandarins, they of course would tell the story in such a manner, as to make it appear that we were prisoners of war.

Note 2, *Page* 13.

In Mrs. Noble's letter, which was published in the " Indian News," it is stated by her that she passed the wreck twice on the 16th, and spoke to us ; but as we left it on the night of the 15th, they must have been Chinese she saw, and whom she at a distance mistook for the crew.

NOTE 3, *Page* 20.

Syrang is the head or chief of every party of
Lascars, and has under him one or more assist-
ants, called Tyndals, according to the number of
his men; he receives the pay, and manages the
affairs of the whole party.

NOTE 4, *Page* 40.

I saw this kind of hall in every house I entered, and at the time imagined that it was dedicated to the Chinese penates; but I have
since found, from " Davis's Chinese," that it is
called the " Hall of Ancestors ;" so throughout
my story I have given it its right name.

NOTE 5, *Page* 44.

This was the compradore, or purveyor, who
had been kidnapped before I left Chusan, so
that he must have been some time in imprisonment. He had been brought with the fleet from
Macao, to act as an interpreter and purveyor.

NOTE 6, *Page* 46.

These Lascars had been captured at different
times at Chusan, whilst engaged in getting fresh

water for their ships. I believe there were regular bands of Chinese round the place, who
seized every foreigner they found wandering
at a distance from his party. One of the people,
belonging to a man-of-war in the harbour, having sauntered some little distance from his companions, was suddenly seized, and was being
dragged off with a rope round his neck. Fortunately for him, his comrades were near, and,
hearing the noise, went immediately to his
rescue, and turned the tables upon the Chinese;
for, taking their weapons from them, they very
soon drove them off, killing several in the skir-
mish. It was by one of these bands that Captain Anstruther was taken.

Note 7, *Page* 49.

The tails, of which they are so exceedingly
proud, are, with many of them, formed mostly of
false hair and silk, plaited together. To be deprived of this ornament is, I believe, almost as
great a disgrace as can befall them.

K

NOTE 8, *Page* 66.

In our close confinement we could see nothing of their religious ceremonies; once or twice, however, I saw our old jailer making his offerings to his gods. The domestics having placed three tables in different parts of the yard, (one being exactly before our window,) ranged round the edge of each nine basins, with chopsticks to all; they then filled the cups with hot rice, and covered the tables with plates of pork, fish, and vegetables, and by the side of every table placed a pile of thin paper. Before each of these tables the old gentleman knelt three times, bowing his head to the ground thrice each time; after this he filled a small cup with samshu, and setting fire to the heap of paper, sprinkled the samshu over the blaze. When he had prostrated himself before all the tables, and burnt the three heaps, he retired to his apartment, and the servants removed the whole apparatus. I suppose his devotions had made him charitable; for all the good things he had prepared for his deities, he distributed amongst us poor prisoners. Several of the respectable people had at various times asked me by signs if the cross were my religion, to which I of course replied in the affirmative.

NOTE 9, *Page* 75.

I think that the Lascars' custom of eating with their hands, in some measure caused the Chinese to treat them with more severity, than they did the Europeans. In lifting the rice to their mouths they generally spilt a little, and there was always some left on the floor after meals; this seemed to shock the Chinese excessively, and the jailer told us " that lightning would fall from heaven, and destroy those who wasted God's bounties."

THE END.

LONDON:
PRINTED BY G. J. PALMER, SAVOY STREET.

For EU product safety concerns, contact us at Calle de José Abascal, 56–1°,
28003 Madrid, Spain or eugpsr@cambridge.org.

www.ingramcontent.com/pod-product-compliance
Ingram Content Group UK Ltd.
Pitfield, Milton Keynes, MK11 3LW, UK
UKHW012339130625
459647UK00009B/407